MIGHTY MUSCLE CARS

DODGE CHALLENGER

Rachael L. Thomas

Big Buddy Books

An Imprint of Abdo Publishing
abdobooks.com

abdobooks.com

Published by Abdo Publishing, a division of ABDO, PO Box 398166, Minneapolis, Minnesota 55439.

Printed in the United States of America, North Mankato, Minnesota
082020
012021

THIS BOOK CONTAINS RECYCLED MATERIALS

Design: Christa Schneider, Mighty Media, Inc.
Production: Mighty Media, Inc.
Editor: Megan Borgert-Spaniol

Cover Photograph: Shutterstock Images

Interior Photographs: Ammar Shaker/Wikimedia Commons, p. 5; Bull-Doser/Wikimedia Commons, pp. 18, 19; Derwin Edwards/Pexels, pp. 26, 27, 29 (2019); dodge challenger1/Flickr, pp. 14, 15, 29 (2008); Greg Larson/Pexels, pp. 20, 21; Harris & Ewing/Wikimedia Commons, pp. 9, 28 (1928); Herranderssvensson/Wikimedia Commons, pp. 10, 11; Mic/Flickr, pp. 24, 25; Mr.choppers/Wikimedia Commons, pp. 13, 28 (1978); Shutterstock Images, pp. 4, 7, 21, 22, 23, 28, 29; Ted Van Pelt/Wikimedia Commons, pp. 16, 17, 29 (2010)

Design Elements: Shutterstock Images

Library of Congress Control Number: 2020931635

Publisher's Cataloging-in-Publication Data
Names: Thomas, Rachael L., author.
Title: Dodge Challenger / by Rachael L. Thomas
Description: Minneapolis, Minnesota : Abdo Publishing, 2021 | Series: Mighty muscle cars | Includes online resources and index
Identifiers: ISBN 9781532193255 (lib. bdg.) | ISBN 9781098211899 (ebook)
Subjects: LCSH: Muscle cars--Juvenile literature. | Motor vehicles--Juvenile literature. | Automobiles--Customizing--Juvenile literature. | Hot rods--Juvenile literature.
Classification: DDC 629.222--dc23

CONTENTS

READY, SET, CHALLENGER!

A Mopar Dodge Challenger Drag Pak and a Challenger Hellcat roll toward the starting line. The drivers rev their engines. The lights turn green, and the cars take off down the drag strip!

The Hellcat gets a quick start, but the Drag Pak picks up speed. It's a cool win for the Drag Pak at just under 11 seconds!

DID YOU KNOW?

In a drag race, two cars race on a straight track called a drag strip. Most drag strips are one-eighth mile (0.2 km) or one-quarter mile (0.4 km) long.

CHALLENGER
MOPAR
MOPAR
OPAR
Hoosier

AMERICAN MUSCLE

The Dodge Challenger has long been a favorite muscle car. Muscle cars are American high-performance cars. They are built for power and speed.

The first muscle car came out in 1949. Muscle cars soon became widely popular in the 1960s. They were made for drag racing. But most could also be driven on city streets.

DODGE CHALLENGER FAST FACTS

Manufacturer: Chrysler

First model year: 1970

Top speed: 203 miles per hour (327 km/h)

Top horsepower: 797 hp

Top acceleration: 0 to 60 miles per hour (96 km/h) in 3.7 seconds

MICHIGAN BORN

In 1900, brothers Horace and John Dodge founded the Dodge Brothers Company in Detroit, Michigan. In 1928, fellow Detroit automaker Walter Chrysler bought Dodge.

The name *Challenger* first appeared on a special-**edition** model in 1958. The Dodge Silver Challenger Club **Sedan** looked little like the well-known Challenger of today. The model was available for only two years.

Automaker Walter Chrysler

THE FIRST GENERATION

Chrysler **debuted** the first-**generation** Dodge Challenger in 1970. The model had features that are now iconic to the Challenger. These included the front **grille** and four headlights. Buyers could choose six-**cylinder** or eight-cylinder engines. These engines had up to 425 horsepower!

DID YOU KNOW?

Horsepower (hp) is a measure of how powerful an engine is. One hp equals the power needed to lift a 550-pound (249 kg) weight up one foot (0.3 m) in one second.

Paint colors for the 1970 Dodge Challenger included Plum Crazy Purple and Sublime Green.

ENGINE DOWNGRADE

Drivers loved the Challenger's bold **design** and powerful engine. But when a new model arrived in 1978, many fans were **disappointed**.

The second-**generation** Challenger had a smaller, less powerful engine. This was because of new US laws that worked to reduce **pollution**. The new model also had a boxier frame and less sporty design. Fans of the original Challenger had to wait almost 30 years for the much-loved design to reappear.

The second-generation Challenger had a four-cylinder engine. It was much less powerful than the first generation's six- or eight-cylinder engine options.

NEW AND IMPROVED

When the Dodge Challenger came back on the scene, it did not **disappoint**! The third-**generation** Challenger SRT8 **debuted** in 2008 at the Chicago Auto Show.

The new model featured the iconic **design** and bold colors of the first generation. It also once again offered a powerful eight-**cylinder** engine. The all-new Challenger could hit 60 miles per hour (96 km/h) in less than five seconds!

The Challenger is bigger than most muscle cars. Most Challenger models can comfortably seat five people and still reach high speeds!

NASCAR CHAMPION

The third-**generation** Challenger made its racing **debut** in 2010 at **NASCAR's** Nationwide Series. NASCAR drivers Justin Allgaier and Brad Keselowski both drove the new Challenger model. Allgaier won one race. Keselowski won six!

Dodge continued to improve the third generation. The 2011 Challenger offered upgrades to the **suspension**, brakes, and steering. Two years later, the Challenger was fitted with a **GPS** system.

The 2010 Challenger at a NASCAR Nationwide Series event

SPEED DEMON

The limited-**edition** Dodge Challenger SRT Demon **debuted** in 2018. The Demon's engine reached up to 808 horsepower. With special fuel, this number rose to 840!

The Demon reached 60 miles per hour (96 km/h) in just 2.3 seconds. The National Hot Rod Association banned the car from its member tracks. The Demon was simply too fast. In fact, it was the fastest car in the world!

The Demon's engine was fitted with a supercharger. This is a device that pushes more air into the cylinders. This gives the engine more power!

UNDER THE HOOD

DODGE CHALLENGER HELLCAT REDEYE

A year after the Demon **debuted**, the Challenger Hellcat Redeye followed. The 2019 Hellcat Redeye featured updates to the Challenger's **design** and **technology**. The *Los Angeles Times* called the Redeye the "**ultimate** American muscle car."

CAR ENGINES 101

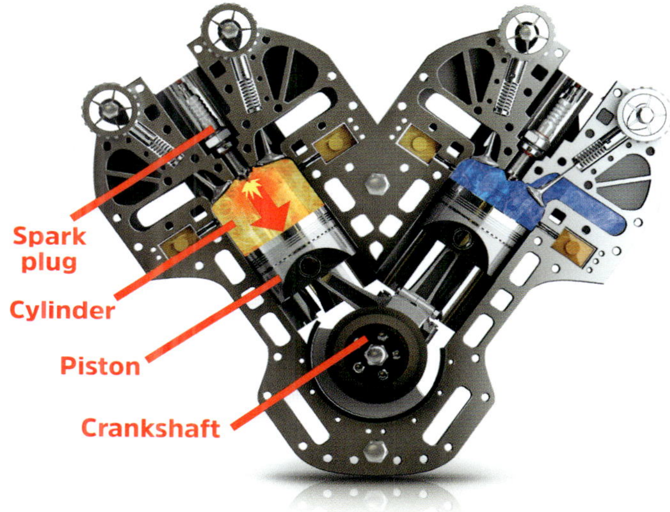

Car engines turn the energy in gasoline into motion. Fuel and air are pumped into the engine's **cylinders**. A spark creates an explosion. The explosion pushes the **piston** down to turn the **crankshaft**. This is a bit like a foot pushing down on a bicycle pedal. At high speed, these explosions happen thousands of times a minute!

RACING FROM YEAR ONE

The Dodge Challenger first hit the track in 1970, the same year it came out. Driver Sam Posey ran the Challenger against other muscle cars at the Trans-American **Sedan** Championship.

Fifty years later, the Challenger is still racing. In 2019, Dodge released the 2020 Mopar Dodge Challenger Drag Pak. This race-ready car was so powerful, it was illegal to drive on the street!

A Dodge Challenger hits the drag strip at the 2019 American Beauty Car Show in Estonia.

SPEEDING ONSCREEN

The Challenger has ruled the movie screen as well as the racetrack. In 1971, it starred in the film *Vanishing Point*. The main character drives a Challenger across the Nevada and Utah deserts.

Nearly 50 years later, the action movie *The Fate of the Furious* featured a 2018 SRT Demon. The Challenger remains a **symbol** of speed, power, and American racing!

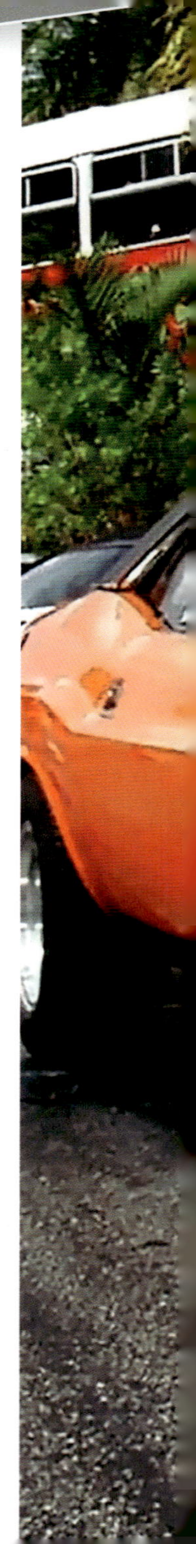

In 2003, the iconic 1970 Challenger appeared in the car-chase movie *2 Fast 2 Furious*.

NEW TECH, NEW DRIVERS

Recent Challenger upgrades have featured new **technologies**, such as backup cameras and touchscreens. But the biggest changes are still to come.

In 2019, Chrysler hinted at one of these changes. Dodge muscle cars may soon be fitted with electric motors! A new age of racers will be hitting the pavement at the wheel of an American icon.

The 2019 Hellcat Redeye

TIMELINE

1900

Horace and John Dodge started the Dodge Brothers Company.

1928

Walter Chrysler purchased Dodge.

1970

Chrysler debuted the first-generation Dodge Challenger.

1978

Chrysler presented the second-generation Dodge Challenger.

2008

The third-**generation** Dodge Challenger SRT8 **debuted** at the Chicago Auto Show.

2010

The third-generation Challenger made its racing debut at **NASCAR's** Nationwide Series.

2018

Dodge came out with the limited-**edition** Challenger SRT Demon.

2019

Dodge debuted the Challenger Hellcat Redeye.

GLOSSARY

crankshaft—a long, metal rod that transfers energy from the engine through the transmission and eventually to the wheels.

cylinder—a shaft in which a piston of an engine moves.

debut—to appear for the first time or present something for the first time. A debut is a first appearance.

design (dih-ZINE)—a plan for how something will appear or work.

disappoint—to make someone feel sad because something hoped for didn't happen.

edition—a version of a product.

generation—a class of objects created from an earlier type.

GPS—a space-based navigation system used to pinpoint locations on Earth.

grille—a metal frame with bars running across it. A grille is used to cover or protect something.

NASCAR—the National Association for Stock Car Auto Racing.

piston—a part in an engine that moves up and down inside the cylinder.

pollution—human waste that dirties or harms air, water, or land.

sedan—a four-door car that has front and back seats and can hold four or more people.

suspension—a system of devices that supports the upper part of an automobile on its axles.

symbol (SIHM-buhl)—an object or mark that stands for an idea.

technology (tehk-NAH-luh-jee)—a capability given by the practical application of knowledge.

ultimate—being the best or greatest.

ONLINE RESOURCES

Booklinks
NONFICTION NETWORK
FREE! ONLINE NONFICTION RESOURCES

To learn more about the Dodge Challenger, please visit **abdobooklinks.com** or scan this QR code. These links are routinely monitored and updated to provide the most current information available.

INDEX